STONE
HOUSES

STONE
HOUSES

Φ

STONE: A REVIVAL

For thousands of years, stone has been synonymous with shelter, protection, and permanence, from megalithic ceremonial sites to classical temples, from humble rural dwellings to imposing fortresses. Highly durable and readily available, stone was quarried, worked, and refined at the hands of skilled stonemasons for millennia, until its primary place as a structural material was superseded during the nineteenth century by reinforced concrete and steel. But with environmental concerns forcing architects and engineers to reevaluate the carbon cost of construction, stone has returned to the spotlight, championed as a more sustainable main material, to be used beyond the mere cladding of a facade.

The projects in this book are testament to the innovation, creativity, and variety that can be achieved through stone construction. A linear limestone home in the shape of a cross occupies a remote plot in rural Mexico (see p. 40), a tiny handmade house nestles between granite boulders on a hillside in Portugal (see p. 50), an unconventional Polish hideaway is built from rock-filled gabion baskets (see p. 62), an angular, wedge-shaped abode in the English countryside is clad almost entirely in rugged flint (see p. 162), and the architectural icon that is Frank Lloyd Wright's Fallingwater pairs local sandstone walls with cantilevered concrete terraces (see p. 118).

Many of the featured projects utilize stone excavated from the site of the building, while others repurpose materials from the derelict structure that originally occupied the plot. A number of painstakingly constructed homes incorporate and reference existing ruins and historic buildings—from a remote Scottish bothy (see p. 234) to a Maltese palazzo (see p. 110)—honoring the craft and construction that enabled these structures to remain standing for centuries. The resilience of natural stone is integral to its appeal both past and present, offering not only a sense of permanence, but a protective shield that fosters a feeling of refuge, no matter how harsh the elements or remote the location. Hobart architects Room 11 harness these qualities in the fort-like home they designed for a particularly exposed plot on Tasmania's Bruny Island (see p. 146), where glazed portions are protected by stacked-stone ramparts. This solid outer shell shelters inhabitants from the strong offshore winds and glaring sunlight, and counteracts the vast openness of the landscape with its reassuring sturdiness.

The enduring strength of stone is, in part, what contributes to its versatility, an attribute that plays out in Malik Architecture's House of Solid Stone (see p. 84), located in an area of India with a long history of sandstone construction. "Rajasthan is synonymous with sandstone as a building material but sadly, over the last few decades, it has been reduced to a cladding medium and its potential as a robust and sustainable structural element has not been explored," says Arjun Malik, principal architect at the Mumbai-based firm. "This house in Jaipur presented us with an opportunity to explore and evolve a method of building that has been prevalent in traditional buildings for centuries."

The architects laid out a simple brief for the House of Solid Stone: no material other than stone could be used in its construction. The design offers a novel take on the traditional load-bearing wall, replacing a thick stone structure with a hollow interlocking system. "This creates a more effective thermal break, provides space to integrate services within the wall cavity, and effectively reduces the material consumption by 30 percent," explains Malik, who enlisted the expertise of local stonemasons, drawing on knowledge handed down through generations. These skills, combined with modern engineering, enabled the entire substructure and superstructure of this house to be crafted solely from stone, as well as the intricate hand-cut external screen that defines its contemporary exterior. Like many other houses in this book that utilize the thermal efficiency of stone, this project benefits from passive energy strategies that regulate interior temperatures throughout the day, making it a comfortable place to live throughout the seasons.

Some advocates of the latent potential of stone believe it has been misrepresented as an expensive material—a reputation that developed as it shifted from a structural element to an external veneer. The environmental credentials of stone as a building material depend on how and where it is quarried, with proximity to the project location being a key element in the building's carbon footprint. While quarrying stone can present certain difficulties, such as obtaining permissions for a new site, as well as operational challenges, experts believe that sourcing can be modernized and future-proofed. Machinery powered by renewable energy plays an important part in this endeavor, as do the conditions for workers, the nature of the waste produced by the process, and the way in which the quarry is returned to the land after use.

Pursuit of perfection is another issue that can detract from stone as a sustainable resource. Unnecessary waste is produced when certain shades or markings are prioritized for a project, and additional manufacturing processes may be employed to finesse appearance. Countless homes in this collection harness the rugged beauty of natural stone, embracing its tonal variations, textures, and sensory appeal. Japanese architect Kengo Kuma has designed an entire complex of villas around the dark and pockmarked volcanic rock that covers Jeju Island in South Korea (see p. 26), while Athens-based Sinas Architects have camouflaged a home within the landscape on the island of Serifos by building ribbon-like structures in the style of the rustic dry stone walls that weave across the hillside (see p. 190).

Other projects that blend their stone construction seamlessly into the surroundings include a bolthole in Idaho, designed by Studio Rick Joy, constructed from local small-rubble granite that echoes the muted colors of the mountainous backdrop (see p. 214). In Marrakesh, Studio KO has devised a home consisting of angular volumes built from local white stone, which appears to spring up like an extension of the ground beneath it (see p. 166). And, taking an unconventional approach to a challenging site, Olson Kundig has carved an entire dwelling into a rocky outcrop in the San Juan Islands in Washington state, creating a cave-like escape largely concealed by the undulating topography of the land (see p. 136). Everything from hand tools to large drills, dynamite, and hydraulic chippers were used to complete the challenging task of embedding this structure into the vast boulders that dominate its coastal plot.

All these projects combine traditional methods and innovative techniques to bring their architects' visions into being, leading one to wonder how building with stone will evolve in the future. One possibility is the use of massive stone, a stonemasonry method originally developed by French architect and urban planner Fernand Pouillon after World War II, where large prefabricated blocks are cut to specific dimensions. In 1948, Pouillon used these pre-cut stone blocks to build the first skyscraper made from load-bearing stone—a 16-story tower that forms part of Marseille's La Tourette housing complex. Fast-forward to the present day, and, thanks to the growing number of architects and engineers backing stone as the future of construction, interest in Pouillon's method is reviving. These machine-cut blocks enable buildings to be rapidly constructed in accordance with architectural plans, speeding up the build process and lowering associated costs. As an added bonus, their substantial size can increase the thermal mass of the walls, improving temperature regulation.

Other sustainable stone construction methods that could shape the buildings of tomorrow include *spolia*—a centuries-old practice that involves reusing the stone from older structures in the construction of new ones—and stone bricks, which require far less energy to manufacture than their traditional clay counterparts. Whatever the future holds for stone in its multitude of forms and functions, it will surely continue to play an integral part in the structures that house us, both urban and rural—whether a private retreat or a sanctuary for the masses, a place of work or of worship, a tower that stretches skyward, or a subterranean bunker. A product of the earth itself, stone is grounding in ways that are both obvious and intangible, providing a sense of connection to the land that is often profoundly lacking in modern life. And, as this inspiring compendium of stone houses proves, its appeal remains as relevant to contemporary architecture as it has been throughout the ages.

TESSA PEARSON

FORT 137

Constructed from stacked blocks of pale-hued limestone that echoes the muted palette of the landscape, the harmonious exterior of this desert home belies the artful interplay of contrasts that lie within. The five-bedroom escape is the work of Nevada studio Daniel Joseph Chenin, which has created a serene retreat for an active, nature-loving family, overlooking Red Rock Canyon, on the edge of the Las Vegas Valley. The design of the project draws inspiration from stone forts built by pioneers across the surrounding desert in the 1800s. Perhaps the most noticeable feature is a central rotunda, which—alongside the rough-hewn limestone walls—counterbalances the otherwise linear exterior of the building. An enticing point of entry, the rotunda offers immediate respite from the heat and harsh winds, leading through to a shaded courtyard that blurs the lines between this luxurious home and its uncompromising environment. Here, a 75-ton (68-metric ton) boulder takes center stage, creating the impression that the house has wrapped itself considerably around this natural feature. Two retractable floor-to-ceiling glass panels peel open the sides of the expansive living area, framing the views and allowing cooling breezes to circulate. The architects utilized various passive cooling techniques—as well as photovoltaic panels, thermal mass, and radiant heating—to reduce the reliance of the home on the grid. Inside, repeated travertine, timber, and brass elements contribute to a refined interior that enhances the impact of the project's robust facade.

SINGLE-FAMILY HOME IN LAS ENCINAS

This imposing stone-clad house in Las Encinas, a neighborhood in the Spanish capital city of Madrid, was inspired by the geological phenomenon of a geode, or hollow rock. Local practice Vicens+Ramos covered the exterior of the building in blasted granite cladding, for a rough and textural outer shell that would conceal a polished interior. The cladding panels create the illusion that enormous blocks of rough-hewn stone have been stacked in asymmetrical formation, giving the structure a pleasingly primitive air that makes the inside all the more surprising. The three-story house is spread across two floors above ground and a basement beneath. In some places, for example where floor-to-ceiling glass walls wrap around a portion of the first floor, the bulk of the structure appears

to be balanced precariously in a playful, top-heavy fashion. These unexpected moments continue inside, as in the living area, where the ceiling finishes abruptly and gives way to a slender double-height void that allows light to flow down from hidden skylights. The rest of the first floor is dedicated to a dining room, family room, office, and a lofty entrance hall leading upstairs.

Eight bedrooms are located on the level above, accessed by a hallway with three openings that take the form of elevated courtyards, set back from the edge of the building, to survey the landscape. From here, you can see the expanse of the large verdant plot on which the buildling sits.

I/S HOUSE

With its seamless, angular facade clad in ivory-colored marble, this triangular abode is a distinctive yet unobtrusive addition to its suburban neighborhood in Savyon, just outside Tel Aviv. Israeli practice Paritzki & Liani's design for I/S House was a response to the trapezoid-shaped site, which became the starting point for the ingenious geometric form of the building, set into the landscape and punctuated with swathes of glass. The architects' brief for this project was to build a 6,458-ft² (600-m²) residence across three stories, while trying to minimize the visual impact of the building on its surroundings. Variations in height play on perspective, which—when combined with the minimalist tapered form and partially subterranean construction—make it hard to discern the full expanse of the home. Built for a family of five, the concept offers numerous tranquil spaces to enjoy privacy, as well as generous communal areas that foster connection. Nature plays a key part here, with apertures and light wells carefully positioned to frame external planting, and landscaping that harnesses the soothing sounds of water. The same Vanilla Ice Turkish marble is used indoors and out, enhancing the fluid link between home and garden. The overall effect lends I/S House an elemental quality: a monolithic structure ensconced in greenery, where sunlight bounces off the smooth stone surfaces and refracts in slender pools of water.

JEJU BALL

Volcanic cones and lava tubes are scattered across the South Korean island of Jeju, which was formed around two million years ago. When Japanese architect Kengo Kuma visited for the first time, he was inspired by the dark and porous basalt rock of the volcanic terrain he found there, and wanted to translate its soft, round qualities into his design for a series of resort villas on the island. The luxury dwellings have been conceived as a collection of pebbles; layers of locally sourced volcanic rubble lie over curved stone roofs made from latticed timber and steel mesh, pierced by rectangular skylights over the rooms. Each roof, clad in the distinctive pockmarked gray stone, arcs down to meet the

earth in places, affording a closer view of the rocks and underlining the building's connection to the earth on which it sits. Inside, where the roof edge juts out beyond the walls, light filters through the rocky canopy, drawing attention to its formation and texture. When viewed from the front, the form becomes clearer: each villa is a two-story residence with wide, covered balconies that cantilever over the lower portions of the buildings. From the rear, it appears that a lava flow following an eruption has enveloped the homes in a dense volcanic scree, largely concealing them from view and embedding the buildings into this spectacular landscape.

VIGLOSTASI RESIDENCE

With its staggered series of white and stone volumes, this coastal home on the island of Syros, Greece was designed to look like a traditional island settlement when viewed from afar. Architecture practice block722, based in Athens, took inspiration from the vernacular buildings found in Aegean villages, with their constellations of low-lying dwellings that pepper the hillsides in the Cyclades, looking out toward the sea. The house was designed for a family of four, as a tranquil escape that emulates the simplicity of the local architecture and makes the most of the island lifestyle. block722 turned to their signature blend of understated architectural forms and modest natural materials

in neutral colors to create a slow-living residence. A network of pathways connect the resulting complex of single-story volumes in white plaster and rustic stone with a succession of gardens and patios. The plan is arranged around a central outdoor space, a nod to the idea of the village plaza, which then leads down toward the pool and main terrace. The complex appears completely at home on its rocky coastal slope, with native planting and living roofs adding to the effect. Inside, light, warm-toned spaces made up of marble, travertine, bamboo, and oak contribute to the sense of quiet luxury that prevails throughout.

THE OLIVE HOUSES

High up in the Tramuntana Mountains, on the Spanish island of Mallorca, two modest stone houses sit amidst a grove of thousand-year-old olive trees. Conceived by Valencia-based studio Mar Plus Ask as a refuge for creatives, the off-grid homes are designed to blend seamlessly into the remote site, preserving its wild, unspoiled quality. The houses sit atop existing terraces of dry-stacked stone that keep their footprint to the minimum. One house utilizes the bones of an existing building, the other has been partially submerged below ground to reduce its impact on the land. Interior walls, floors, and ceilings are clad in colored stucco, in shades of pink and purple to complement the leaves of the surrounding olive trees, the surfaces sloping to create a cave-like atmosphere that enhances the back-to-basics appeal of this mountain sanctuary. The Pink House, as the new structure is called, has been built around an enormous rock and contains a bedroom overlooking the valley. An open fire provides heat in the colder months, while a large skylight punctures the vaulted ceiling, below which an open shower draws filtered rainwater from the roof. The Purple House offers a separate bathroom, and space to cook and dine, equipped with gas burners, a wood-fired oven, and a solar-powered refrigerator. A large frameless opening connects the interior with the ancient trees outside.

ENSO II

When HW Studio Arquitectos embarked on this rural project close to San Miguel de Allende in Mexico, their construction material was an obvious choice: locally quarried limestone. In the Guanajuato region, limestone features in both the architectural and the artisanal, and the architects devised a concept that would pay homage to the cultural significance of the material, the skill involved in building with it, and the mountains surrounding this remote plot. Their design draws from vernacular houses and takes the shape of a cross, with the cruciform layout intended to induce a sense of pilgrimage as residents pass between the various areas of the home, inviting contemplation of the landscape. The four quadrants are delineated by thick stone walls that shelter open-air thoroughfares with uninterrupted sight lines, while the limestone bricks match the color of the terrain, making the house appear as if it has emerged from the ground. Each quadrant has been assigned its own function. One contains the garden that greets the visitor on arrival, the second houses the living accommodation — a one-bedroom structure with the kitchen, dining, and living areas, and the third is for cars. Crouching close to the ground, the low-lying volume emphasizes the undulating topography of the area. The fourth quadrant contains a two-story building housing an office and is the sole vertical element of the project: a deliberate contrast to the wide, uninterrupted horizons.

VILLA NEMES

Built using stone excavated from its hillside location in Liguria in northwest Italy, the design of this villa was inspired by the terraced landscape surrounding it. The secluded home traces the topography of the land, and is made up of two semi-subterranean volumes arranged across a single story, ensconced within the dense vegetation that covers the sloping site. A green roof helps to minimize the visual impact of the building. On one side of the main entrance is an open-plan kitchen, dining, and living area; on the other is a succession of five bedrooms, all of which lead out to the garden. Large apertures feature throughout the house, creating breaks in the stone exterior and affording sight lines to the sea. The window frames are integrated into the structure to reduce their visual impact both inside and out. Sustainability was key to Giordano Hadamik's design, and the placement of the windows to maximize thermal insulation, together with use of solar and other renewable energy sources, allows the house to reach Passivhaus standards. The interior spaces are lined with understated concrete and timber while the unobstrusive window surrounds enhance the views out to the swimming pool, old oak trees, and the Mediterranean landscaping that helps to embed the house within its verdant setting.

CASA DO PENEDO

Sandwiched between four enormous granite boulders, Casa do Penedo, or Boulder House, is an architectural curiosity located on a hilltop outside of Fafe in northern Portugal. It took local engineer Leonel Marques Rodrigues two years to complete the highly unusual home, which he created as an isolated rural retreat for his family. Walls peppered with small windows bridge the gap between the giant rocks, forming a compact two-story house. The man-made elements of the structure are clad in pebbledash to mimic the rough, mottled surface of the large rocks that sit at each corner, while the roof is covered in tiles that blend in with the tones of the stone. Perfectly integrated with the rugged landscape surrounding it, the quirky abode is now a museum and tourist destination, where visitors can explore the rustic, hand-built interior. A tiny kitchen and living area—featuring a large concrete-and-wood sofa—occupy the first floor, while the bedrooms above are accessed via a wooden staircase. Every room in the house has a different shape, determined by the rock formations that enclose it. Despite now being located a stone's throw from a large wind farm, the home remains an off-grid destination, lit by candles after dark. Carved into a rocky outcrop just below Casa do Penedo is a swimming pool with uninterrupted views to the distant mountain ranges.

RESIDENCE 145

Granite segments break up the bright-white frontage of this three-story house in Chandigarh, India, designed by local architecture firm Charged Voids. The same stone features heavily throughout the interior, where a considered layout caters to the needs of a multi-generational family. Connection is at the core of the concept, whether between family members or with the outdoors. Residence 145 features a granite-clad internal courtyard that helps to circulate light and fresh air, aided by punctures in the walls that allow the wind to pass through. An intricate arrangement of solids and voids supports the architects' bid to balance communal and secluded spaces. The first floor comprises an open-plan, double-height living area that flows into a dining space and wraps around the central courtyard, as well as a bedroom for the grandparents. Above are two more bedrooms, and an open kitchen that overlooks the courtyard via a curved wall with a window and glass balustrade. On the third floor, a large, lushly planted terrace offers space to entertain outside. The studio was keen to avoid superfluous ornamentation throughout, working instead with granite tiles in different formats to strengthen the link between inside and out. The focus here is firmly on sensory experience, provided, for example, by the abundant natural light that permeates the home, the scent of the surrounding foliage, and the sound of the water trickling softly in the courtyard.

STONE HOUSE

Perched on a rocky slope overlooking the sea, the exterior of this Menorcan home pairs textural limestone with sections of smooth, pale plaster, a contemporary nod to the vernacular architecture of the Balearic island. Stone House is the work of Barcelona-based Nomo Studio and has been built in much the same way as the ancient limestone walls that border most of the farmland on the island, using stone excavated from the villa's foundations. Despite the client's deep appreciation for Menorca's architectural customs, the studio felt strongly that the design should avoid pastiche. The exterior reinterprets a local construction technique that sees windows and outlines framed in white plaster, resulting in a striking patchwork effect. Inside the six-bedroom home, the cohesive material palette continues with sand-colored concrete, whitewashed walls, and pale pine woodwork. The interior plan revolves around an impressive double-height space at the center of the two-story house, which draws in light and frames the ocean views. On the lower level, sliding glass doors lead out to the garden, where hardy coastal vegetation surrounds a large limestone terrace flanking a swimming pool clad in gray stone. The glazed portions of the house —when combined with flexible shading and the insulation offered by the limestone walls—contribute to a sustainable methodology that achieves the highest ranking in energy performance. The result is a thoughtful and innovative reframe of the island's ancestral architecture.

HOUSE IN THE LANDSCAPE

Gabion baskets filled with local limestone rocks form the walls of this two-story home located in an area of Jurassic highland known as the Kraków-Częstochowa Upland, or Polish Jura. The architects—Kraków-based Kropka Studio—wanted to reflect local building traditions in a contemporary way, as well as to camouflage House in the Landscape within the spectacular surroundings of limestone cliffs, vast rock formations, and towering medieval ruins. Availability of materials, cost, and durability also influenced the choice of the stone-filled, wire-mesh gabions for this four-person family home, which has ample space for large gatherings, as per the client's request. Once the stacked

gabions were secured to insulated structural walls, the house was topped with a graphite-colored, titanium-zinc roof, its sloping design dictated by local building regulations. Behind the robust facade, a bright and spacious interior is arranged in a flowing, L-shaped plan. A double-height kitchen and living area occupying a large portion of the building is the highlight. Beyond this—extending into the garden—is the master bedroom and bathroom, with contrasting timber cladding on the outside. Two additional bedrooms can be found on the level above, accessed by a steel staircase with cantilevered stair treads in a linear design that nods to the home's tough, no-frills exterior.

THE PARCHMENT WORKS

In a rural corner of Northamptonshire, in the East Midlands of England, an extension made from corten steel, reclaimed bricks, and glass has been slotted inside the tumbledown ruins of a former parchment factory, dating back to the 1600s, and old cattle shed. The homeowner felt the previously derelict structure, although historic and a scheduled monument, was a barrier to maximizing the potential of their existing Grade II-listed, double-fronted Victorian property, and brought in London studio Will Gamble Architects to devise a solution. Rather than demolishing the ruins, as per the client's initial brief, the architects came up with a sensitive intervention that would celebrate what was left of the factory's limestone and ironstone walls. Two lightweight volumes were delicately inserted inside the crumbling masonry shell, built from up-cycled materials largely found on site, in a cost-effective and sustainable construction approach. The material palette, which also included oversized timber joists, was chosen to reflect the home's rural context, ensuring the new additions did not feel out of step with their immediate or wider surroundings. In the new kitchen, the old stone walls have been re-pointed and limewashed, creating a softer appearance that contributes to a cohesive feel. Sleek, contemporary cabinetry offsets the irregular, somewhat disordered elements of the ruin, continuing the harmonious balance of ancient and modern.

ARMADALE RESIDENCE

Built from 260 tons (236 metric tons) of pale-hued granite, the exterior of this three-story home in Armadale, a suburb of Melbourne, has an air of lightness that seems to contradict its construction. The client was drawn to the solidity of natural stone but concerned that its visual heaviness would feel overpowering. Local studio B. E. Architecture chose the silvery gray split-faced granite for its characteristic of reflecting light, to simulate a cloud-like appearance that would offset the formidable bulk of the stone structure. Striking a delicate balance between permanence and playfulness, the textural facade serves to soften the sharp lines of the stacked volumes that make up the rectilinear building. Three different forms of granite were chosen for the construction: split-face granite for the exterior; Torino granite for both indoor and outdoor tiles; and Fallow granite for the floors and walls of an impressive master en suite, where a custom bath and basin have also been crafted from solid blocks of stone. Working closely with highly skilled builders and stone masons, B. E. Architecture were able to draw out subtle variations from their materials, changing the finish of the stone to make it suitable for different applications. The three varieties of granite form a cohesive thread that runs throughout the house, contributing to a timeless scheme that thoughtfully marries inside and out.

STONE HOUSE

Located in the Spanish city of Cáceres, which boasts a rich and varied blend of historical architectural vernaculars, this stone home is a distinctly uncomplicated addition to the mix. The cube-like structure is built from local quartzite, and displays a pleasing uniformity that complements its unostentatious construction. Four walls measuring 52 ft (16 m) in length delineate a square floor plan, while each facade is punctuated by three large windows, contributing to the visual symmetry. The apertures, framed in Extremadura granite, another locally quarried stone, are fitted with sliding doors that connect the home with the generous garden that surrounds it. Beyond the entrance, a small courtyard creates a pause between outside and in. Within the four walls, the home is divided into a series of nine smaller cubes, each dedicated to a different function. These identically proportioned spaces contain bedrooms, living areas, the kitchen, and a dining room, with bathrooms and closets placed in between. Oak boards line the lower portions of the rooms, concealing the building's service elements, with white concrete above, elevating the height of the ceilings and giving the interior an airy feel. The central space within the first floor of the cube is given over to a futuristic spiral staircase, which sweeps downward, connecting the two levels of the house.

FAIRYLAND GUORUI VILLAS

Ridged stone cladding covers the fluid exteriors of the homes that make up the enchantingly named Fairyland Guorui Villa complex, located at the meeting point of two rivers in Beijing. Scattered along the water's edge, this development of ethereal homes was designed by Dutch architecture and design firm UNStudio, who oriented the villas toward different views of the natural landscape and the intersecting network of tree-lined boulevards. Alike inside but unique externally, each villa is defined by different combinations of features integrated into their facades. These include recessed balconies, bay windows, terraces, and roof-top gardens, as well as overhanging canopies that look as though they have been carved out of solid stone. The undulating walls of the homes both unite and differentiate the various residences, avoiding the homogeneity that often afflicts new-build housing developments.

The distinctive cladding selected by UNStudio is made from recycled stone, which is powdered and reconstituted. The sinuous nature of the exteriors is integral to the design, creating rhythms from one elevation to the next, and the slender forms of the stone make this possible. At the core of the concept of this newly constructed neighborhood is the desire to foster a sense of connection between its residents and the outdoors. The architects used the twisting, textured surfaces to reference the mountains that form the backdrop to the complex, while the clay-colored facades enhance the link between the built and the natural environment.

HOUSE OF SOLID STONE

From the hefty blocks that make up its walls to the intricate screen that clads the facade, every element of this home has been crafted from locally sourced sandstone. The house is located in Jaipur, in the state of Rajasthan, an area once synonymous with sandstone construction. Mumbai-based architects Malik Architecture chose to explore and evolve this sustainable material—which has been used in traditional construction for centuries—and decided to exclude all other building materials from the project. Observing these time-old techniques through a new lens, the studio opted to reengineer the robust, load-bearing stone walls to create a hollow, interlocking system with the double function of providing an effective thermal break and allowing services to be integrated within the wall cavity. Inside and out, the four-story house showcases the versatility of sandstone and the expertise of local stonemasons, whose skills were integral to achieving the different formats and finishes. Sections built using riven sandstone are juxtaposed with sleeker surfaces, while angular elements sit alongside round windows and vaulted ceilings. Arranged around a courtyard that narrows as it weaves its way through the house, the design utilizes various voids to bring in light without exposing the interior to the full heat of the sun. Each of its deep-set windows is covered by shuttered apertures in the hand-cut screen, which offer shade and privacy.

RUINS STUDIO

Built within the ruins of an eighteenth-century farmhouse near Dumfries, the design of this remote Scottish home references the numerous historical alterations to the original building. Paris-based Nathanael Dorent Architecture and London-based Lily Jencks Studio together devised this sequence of contrasting materials and geometries to create a contemporary counterpoint to the old stone walls. The house is conceived as a series of layers, the outer layer being the existing stone walls, which dictate the locations of the large windows and doors. Within this shell sits a dark, rubber-clad, pitched-roofed structure that in turn conceals an unexpected curved interior composed of insulating recycled polystyrene blocks set into a gridded wooden frame. The bright white walls—covered in Glass Reinforced Plastic—add to the sense of contrast set in motion by the three different layers.

The complete assemblage of visually opposing elements demonstrates how the narrative of a building can change over time. Within the curvilinear interior, the floor plan widens and narrows to define separate areas, while the structural grid is visible in places, creating shelving and seating. The rustic stone walls make an appearance too, forming a partition between the kitchen and living area. Both of these spaces feature wood-burning stoves to warm the house, which employs Passivhaus principles. The completed home offers a dynamic sensory experience, with carefully framed views across the open countryside and a cocoon-like quality that is both intriguing and comforting.

E/C HOUSE

Set on the edge of Pico Island in the Azores, a
group of volcanic islands in the North Atlantic, this
home started with a ruin composed of dark, basalt
rock. Setúbal-based practice SAMI-arquitectos
was enlisted to build a new holiday home on the
hillside plot. Keen to retain the stone walls of the
existing building, their solution was to construct a
clean-lined and compact residence inside the ruin.
The cladding of pale concrete panels enhances
the contrast between the new and old structures.
The 1,668-ft^2 (155-m^2) home is set into the hillside,
the lower floor accommodating bedrooms and
bathrooms, while above, a kitchen-diner, living
room, and numerous terraces capitalize on the
elevated position and allow for quiet moments of
contemplation. The newly constructed volumes
feature wide apertures, some aligned with breaks
in the original walls, enabling views toward the
sea and verdant coastline. Other windows frame
the walls themselves, drawing the eye toward the
rugged forms of the volcanic rocks. Areas where
the structure of the old building has completely
disintegrated allow light to flood into the interior,
where a white-and-wood scheme complements
the pared-back aesthetic of the architecture.
The airy ambience inside continues the appealing
incongruity of the newly built and pre-existing
elements, heightening the dramatic visual effect
of the dark and pitted stone walls that surround
the minimalist abode.

JORDI AND ÁFRICA'S HOME

Designed by local practice TEd'A arquitectes, this cuboid-shaped home built from *marés*, a local sandstone, is located on the Spanish island of Mallorca. The compact 3,466-ft² (311-m²) house was built on a corner plot formerly occupied by a single-story dwelling in the village of Montuïri, creating a larger home with a more functional layout, as well as an exterior patio that benefits from the sunny climate. Eschewing the need for a dominant facade, the uniform shape was chosen to give equal importance to each external wall of the house. The construction of these walls was key to the design process: the architects reused the original sandstone recovered from the demolition of the old structure, the weathered and patinated blocks giving character to the new build, as well as highlighting the traditional skills of the craftsmen who had carved and chiseled it. Newer pieces were sourced from the same quarry as the existing stone to supplement the construction. Rather than diluting the effect of the older, more textural stone, the new sandstone adds subtle impact; it has been layered in around the old, defining details such as the window openings and the roof line. The effect is a modern yet timeless building that brings new relevance to and showcases ancient skills.

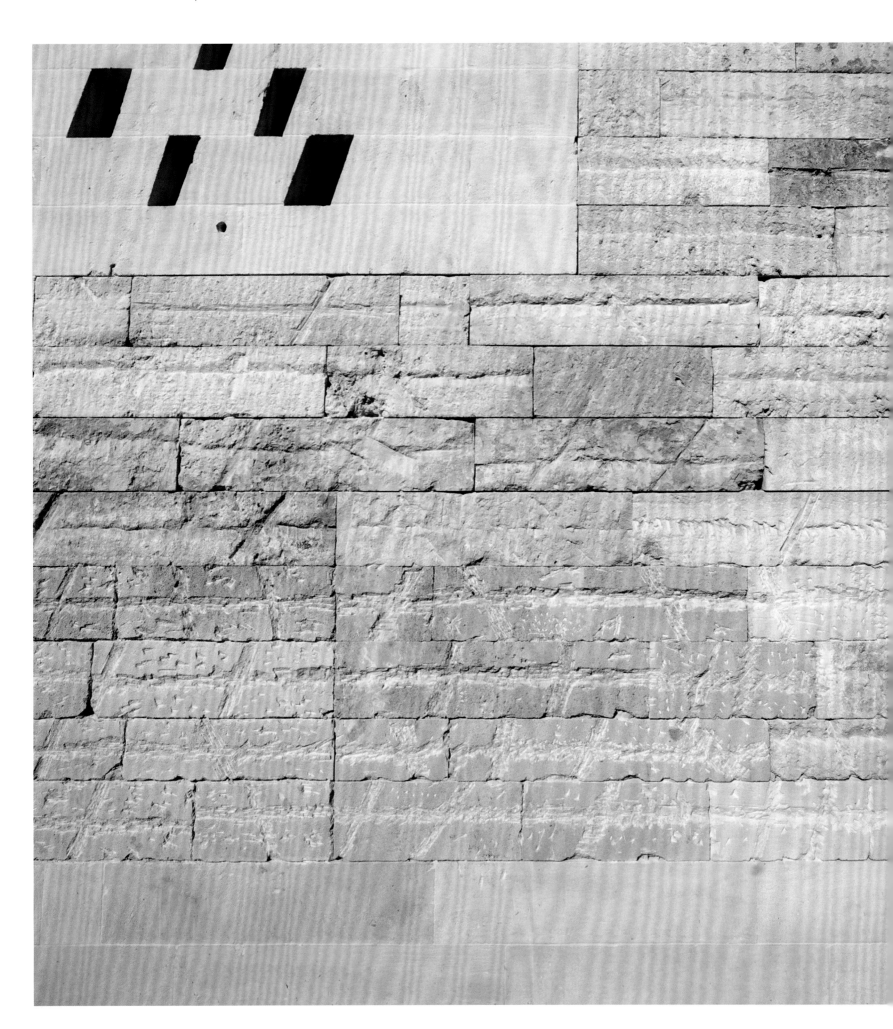

TAKAMINE HOUSE

When Japanese architect Tomoaki Uno was commissioned to build a home in the city of Nagoya, Japan, using dry stone construction methods, he searched for a respectful way to employ this ancient method of Japanese masonry, originally used for castle foundations and stone walls. Drawing inspiration from a photograph of the ancient stone pyramids at Tenayuca, an Aztec archaeological site located in the Valley of Mexico, Uno opted to use it for the larger volume of the residence, resulting in the distinctive pyramid that forms part of Takamine House, which contains the client's secluded study. Beside it sits a concrete volume that houses the living spaces and bedrooms. The rugged and irregular granite stones that form the pyramid's walls offset the bunker-like feel of the adjacent concrete structure and hint at the poetic nature of this inward-looking home, which is arranged around a courtyard and water garden. The light penetrating the living areas is in stark contrast to the moody sanctuary found within the pyramid: a tranquil space with a fireplace and a spiritual atmosphere that reflects its unconventional inspiration.

THE COACH HOUSE

Stone cladding in a weave design crowns this extension to an old coach house in Balzan, Malta, added as part of an extensive renovation project by local practice AP Valletta. Originally a single-story service building for the adjacent eighteenth-century palazzo, the dilapidated structure would clearly need a huge amount of work to transform it into a functional residence, but redeeming features such as the solid-stone construction and soaring ceilings—some of which are more than 13 ft (4 m) high—revealed the potential of the building. The architects believe that certain elements, like a large former mill room, could predate the palazzo itself, and were careful to preserve as much of the existing building as possible. They wanted to create a contemporary design for the new owners, while responding to the historical ties with the palazzo. Their solution was to extend upward, placing a new volume atop the old building to house a master suite and additional bedroom. The stone cladding that appears to weave its way across the exterior of the second level was chosen to reference local building techniques while giving the facade a contemporary edge. All structural interventions protect the integrity of the existing building, with new additions designed to be removed or reversed should the need arise.

VILLA MOLLI

Bluish-gray moraine stone clads the exterior of this home on the banks of Lake Como, echoing the serene shades of the water below and contrasting with the warmer tones of the more traditional residences that surround it. Villa Molli was designed by local architect Lorenzo Guzzini and consists of a central single-story structure flanked by two taller volumes located on a steep section of land that divides the forest from the lake. Once agricultural, this area has been reclaimed by mountain vegetation springing up between the historic stone buildings. The traditional neighboring house informs the appearance of Villa Molli, in the two larger sections that bookend the central living and dining area, and in the stone cladding itself, which was inspired by regional construction techniques, and yet innovative details like the unusual stepped roofs made from the same slabs that form the ridges in the facade define the project.

The design has kept site excavation to a minimum, and the building is spread over multiple levels that traverse the sharp incline of the terrain. A narrow terrace divides the living areas from an infinity pool, with steep, terraced gardens heading down to the lakeside beyond. Moving through the angular, atmospheric interior, the outlook is ever-changing, with views across the lake, taking in water, sky, and Como's only island, Isola Comacina.

FALLINGWATER

An architectural icon and designated landmark, Frank Lloyd Wright's Fallingwater needs no introduction. Alongside New York's Guggenheim Museum, it is perhaps the American architect and designer's most celebrated achievement, and embodies his pioneering organic architecture style. Built in 1935 for Edgar and Liliane Kaufmann, the house sits atop a waterfall in Mill Run in a densely forested corner of Pennsylvania deemed the perfect place for a weekend retreat. Wright said that he wanted the Kaufmanns to live with the waterfall, rather than just look at it, and he set about making the waterfall an integral part of the architecture. Designed as an extension of the landscape, the house is constructed from locally quarried sandstone laid to imitate the natural stone ledges that jut out of the riverbank. Enormous cantilevered terraces extend out over the waterfall, crafted from cement, sand, and rounded river gravel. On the first floor, a hatch opens onto a suspended stairway leading down to the water below. Inside, an abundance of textural stone elements provide a link to the exterior; these include irregular flagstone floors, as well as walls, pillars, and hearths crafted from jagged sandstone. The Kaufmanns donated their beloved home to the Western Pennsylvania Conservancy in 1963. Fallingwater is now a carefully preserved museum that needs constant specialized maintenance to protect the structure, so that visitors can continue to appreciate the artistry of its iconic design.

CASA FLY

Slovakian studio Beef Architekti were keen to embrace the vernacular Mallorcan architecture in this project on the largest of Spain's Balearic islands, and their modern stone house showcases traditional materials and local building techniques. Dry stone walls in a style typical of the region make up much of the textural facade, which also features large glazed portions that open the interior to the garden, terrace, and swimming pool. All of the windows are set back from the exterior, taking advantage of the shade created by the concrete slabs that run horizontally across the building, helping to keep the house cool. Folding wooden shutters offer further protection from the sun, a contemporary interpretation of another time-honored Mallorcan building custom, as well as privacy from the street. Narrow vertical slats allow air to circulate even when the shutters are closed, and create delicate shadows throughout the restrained interior. In the living spaces, stone is combined with a neutral palette of lime plaster, wood and concrete providing an understated canvas to highlight the artistry of custom-made elements and handmade pieces. Each level of the house benefits from different views of the island, enhanced by the large windows. On the first floor, the sea provides a backdrop to the pool and garden, while from the bedrooms and bathrooms on the level above, a nearby city can be seen through the pine trees, illuminated after dark.

ECHEGARAY HOUSE

Traditionally, homes built in this part of the State of Mexico feature communal areas on the lower floors with private spaces above. Local architecture practice PPAA decided to reverse this construct, placing the bedrooms on the central level of this partially submerged home. The incline of the hillside plot means that a portion of the house—an unassuming black box when viewed from the street—is set into the slope. The first and second floors of Echegaray House are constructed from concrete blocks, the former containing a parking garage that faces the street. On the central bedroom level, the jagged forms of the excavated rock surrounding the house are visible through floor-to-ceiling windows, making a feature out of the rugged terrain, which feels both intriguing and unexpected given the urban location of the home.

The transition from private to public spaces is enhanced by a change in atmosphere, with light flooding in through a skylight as you ascend through the house by a circulation space that avoids the private areas. The architects' inverted layout allows the living and dining areas on the top floor to open onto a roof terrace to the front that offers panoramic views across the city skyline, and a garden to the rear. Designed to keep excavation of the site to a minimum, the arrangement makes clever use of a tricky plot, while at the same time anchoring the home within the geography of its terrain.

CASA WARD

Staggered in a formation that its architect likens to an extended telescope, this house stretches across a hilltop plot facing Le Marche's Sibillini Mountains. The area is filled with the ruins of old stone farmhouses, destroyed by a series of earthquakes that struck the region in 2016. This stone-and-concrete home has been built on the site of one such ruin, and is the work of Paris-based studio Carl Fredrik Svenstedt Architects. Sympathetically conceived yet contemporary in design, Casa Ward has a concrete frame dictated by strict seismic regulations. This frame is anchored to the slope to protect the structure from any movement below ground, and partially concealed by walls of brick and stone that complement, rather than conceal, its presence. Material salvaged from the remains of the original farmhouse was used to build the walls, an ode to the past that is, crucially, fit for the future. The home's telescopic design, which extends from east to west, is oriented toward the mountain range and comprises a series of open courtyards that make the most of the awe-inspiring surroundings. Inside, the reclaimed stone is the hero of the material palette, but the walls also incorporate sections of concrete, which frame and reflect the wider dialogue between tradition and innovation throughout the project. Large windows puncture the stone-clad walls, where the mountains are framed like a living landscape painting.

THE PIERRE

Building a house within an immense stone outcrop is no easy task, but Seattle firm Olson Kundig were undeterred by the challenge when they embarked on this project in the San Juan Islands, an archipelago in Washington state, USA. The owner's appreciation for the view from the peak of the rock formation inspired the design of the home, which had to be carved into the landscape using large drills, dynamite, hydraulic chippers, and a selection of hand tools. Conceived as a concrete bunker hidden within the towering, protective walls formed by the outcrop, the house—named The Pierre after the French word for stone—both blends in with and stands out from its surroundings. Exposed rock makes an appearance in different parts of the interior, a reminder of the unique situation and construction. Stone excavated from the site was repurposed as crushed aggregate in the concrete flooring that runs throughout. The main level of the house features an impressive indoor–outdoor living space with a central hearth carved out of the existing rock. Here, a vast steel-and-glass door pivots open to connect the interior with a seating area outside, where a second fireplace mirrors the placement of the internal hearth. From within the living space as well as outside on the terrace, the spectacular scenery that led to the ambitious design of this island retreat can be admired.

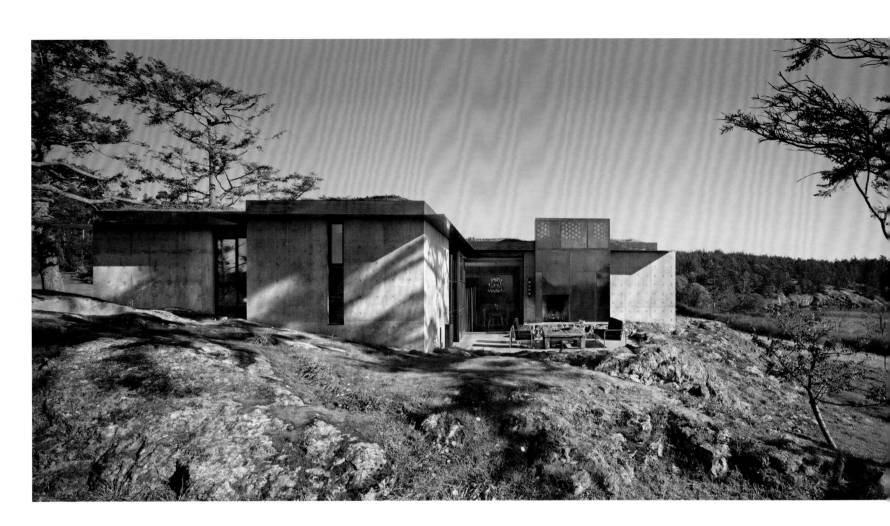

BOX HOUSE

A contemporary red-brick structure has been slotted inside the traditional stone walls of this ruined house in Romarigães, a rural village in northern Portugal. The visual tension between old and new is deliberate: architect Tiago Sousa's aim was to reflect the conflict that arises between past and present when faced with the task of reimagining an old building for modern life. Set across two levels, the project makes use of existing apertures in the original exterior walls, so the footprint remains unchanged. Additional space has been carved out on the second floor, where the new brick structure protrudes from the old granite shell, creating covered sun terraces for the two bedrooms. Inside, the material scheme is intentionally restrained. White walls and timber floors extend throughout the interior, where sections of Sapele wood cladding conceal doorways for uniformity. Details of the original stone structure can still be seen here and there, where the new windows have been designed around the old openings. At the center of Box House, a curvilinear staircase made from concrete separates the kitchen and dining areas from the living room, all of which occupy a single open-plan space. The living space is connected to the outside via a glass sliding door, where a concrete overhang covers a small terrace and provides shelter from the intensity of the sun.

D'ENTRECASTEAUX HOUSE

On a wind-buffeted plot on Tasmania's remote and beautiful Bruny Island, D'Entrecasteaux House hunkers down within its protective, stone-walled shell. Hobart architecture firm Room 11 devised the courtyard surrounding the house as a shield against the elements, and as a veil, to help it blend into the vast openness of the landscape. Within the reassuringly solid stone ramparts that encase this modern fortress sits a glass-fronted structure. It overlooks the D'Entrecasteaux Channel, from which the house takes its name. Occasional breaks in the exterior walls create sightlines to the sea and opportunities for quiet contemplation, while maintaining the barrier that serves to break the offshore winds. The interior provides a startling contrast to the expansive nature of the surroundings: the walls are clad in black-stained wood, creating a cocooning retreat. The darkness is deliberate, to provide relief from the blisteringly bright Tasmanian sunlight, which is compounded by the glare reflecting off the water. The rich-black tones of the timber also highlight the textural qualities of the gray stone walls, as well as the vibrancy of the sea and sky beyond them. The concept soothes inhabitants on a deeper, more primal level too, creating a sense of refuge within the wildness of this isolated plot situated on an island accessible only by boat.

NCAVED

Set into a scrub-covered hillside in a small, secluded cove, the inventive design of this sunken home seeks to shelter inhabitants from the strong north winds while preserving the spectacular sea views. Working with granite excavated from the site, Athens studio MOLD Architects chose to submerge the house within the sloping coastline, rather than arrange the spaces at ground level where they would be more exposed. The architects describe the concept of NCaved as a three-dimensional chessboard of solids and voids enclosed by dry stone walls that draw the eye out to the horizon. These jagged borders help to anchor this overtly contemporary cave-like home within the craggy coastal landscape. The stone walls extend all the way through to the back of the structure, contributing a sense of ruggedness to an otherwise minimalist interior palette of exposed concrete and slatted timber. These materials were selected to recreate the feel of a natural cavity carved out within the hillside. Once inside, clean lines and fuss-free forms ensure that nothing obstructs the views. The rear windows frame indoor gardens, allowing light and air to circulate, while the entire front section of the house is fully open to the east. Here, floor-to-ceiling glass doors allow the interior spaces to flow out onto partially covered terraces protected from the wind by the rocky hillside.

HELLER LANE

Originally designed in 1978 by Modernist architect Norman Jaffe, this home in East Hampton, New York, features a distinctive shingle roof and walls of stacked Tennessee sandstone in dramatically varied shades. Heller Lane is built in Jaffe's self-described Zeus style, taking inspiration from the sea and sky, and the large sand dunes that edge the Long Island coast, where he transformed much of the vernacular architecture throughout his career.

The home had been subjected to several incongruous interior renovations over the years, something that New York architect Neil Logan sought to rectify. He set to work reorganizing the interior, leaving the exterior largely untouched.

To improve the flow and circulation of the floor plan, Logan made the bold decision to remove one of two original masonry fireplaces. The windowless facade to the front was preserved, while elsewhere, large windows and glass sliding doors were introduced to open the kitchen, dining, and living spaces up to the garden and the ocean beyond. Oak walls, floors, and joinery are a harmonious addition to the sensitively updated interior, which flows out onto a newly decked courtyard in one direction and to a swimming pool and guest house in another. Two original bedrooms remain downstairs, while above, four new bedrooms were added, including a master suite with a wraparound terrace affording a view across the dunes and out to sea.

FLINT HOUSE

Informed by their unique geo-archaeological approach to architecture, London- and Madrid-based practice Skene Catling de la Peña conceived this home as a flint landscape that has been carved away to form a dwelling. The studio was enlisted to build a three-bedroom house in the grounds of Waddesdon Manor in Buckinghamshire, in southeast England, an area situated on a great seam of chalk that runs from the White Cliffs of Dover all the way up to the Norfolk coast. Wedge-shaped, with a stepped roof that provides access to its highest point, the building is a striking addition to the rolling countryside around it. The main house contains a kitchen, dining room, living area, library, study, and bedrooms, while a separate annex studio mirrors

the sharp incline of the sloped roof. The exterior of the angular build is clad almost entirely in flint, an ancient form of quartz found in chalk. The stone cladding transitions from coarse, black flint at the base to smooth, matt chalk higher up, creating a subtle gradation of color across the facade. Terrazzo tiles have been used for the roof and the balconies, which look out onto the wide, green landscape. Chalk-covered nodules of bone-like, raw flint line the walls of a water-channel that bisects this contemporary grotto, which features a double-sided fireplace. Beyond this, floors of dark, serpentine stone contrast with pure white walls, giving the interior a serene feel, embedded in nature.

VILLA DL

The orientation of this stone villa set on a sandy, weather-beaten plot close to the Atlantic coastline was dictated by the prevailing northeast winds that batter the terrain. Built from local white stone that nods to the surrounding dry stone boundary walls, Villa DL is located on the outskirts of a quiet rural village, with views across a vast uninhabited landscape to the west. Parisian architecture practice Studio KO devised linear stone volumes that appear to emerge from the ground in a geometric formation. Taking aesthetic cues from traditional neighboring farmhouses, the villa comprises four blocks arranged around a central courtyard giving protection from the strong winds, and making the most of the unspoiled western vista. A considered material palette allows a fluid dialogue between inside and out, as well as ensuring the house feels at home in its unforgiving environment. Benslimane cleaved stone complements the white stone walls, while concrete clads the vaulted ceilings in the living area. Elsewhere, ceilings have been crafted from thuja beams and laurel logs, and window lintels feature timber salvaged from old boats. Interspersed with a collection of vintage and modern pieces, handmade furnishings, such as wicker pendant lights, braided rugs, raw wood tables, and traditional stools with woven palm seats, enliven the minimalist interior and showcase the local craft skills.

CASA PASTRANA

A pink-hued home comprised of two similar yet contrasting volumes, Casa Pastrana is located in the foothills of the Sierra de las Moreras, a coastal mountain range not far from Murcia in southern Spain. The project involved extending and refurbishing an existing building, and local architect Pepa Díaz looked to the archetypal Mediterranean house found throughout Levante, the eastern region of the Iberian peninsula. A new extension now sits alongside the original stone structure, built with local quartzite. The twin volumes are defined by their angular geometry, as well as the interplay of opposing textures; clay covers the larger of the two, while stone recovered from the building works was used in the restoration of the refurbished section. The architect also introduced timber elements and

an untreated terracotta floor, completing a pared-back and sustainable material palette intended to help her client detach from day-to-day life.

With its sealed yet breathable construction, the house retains a pleasant temperature in the summer, without the need for air conditioning. A wood-burning stove is the sole source of heat when the temperature drops in winter. This back-to-basics approach to comfort reflects the architect's wish to connect the inhabitants to the original essence of the house: an unobtrusive stone dwelling that occupies a peaceful plot amidst fields and linear dry stone terraces, at the base of the dramatic sierra.

THE TRUFFLE

At first glance, this unusual dwelling in Costa da Morte, on Spain's Galician coast, appears to have been whittled out of a huge boulder and deposited in a prime spot overlooking the ocean. In fact, Madrid-based Ensamble Studio built the entire structure in situ from scratch, using a series of unconventional techniques designed to simulate the process of mineral formation. The construction team began by excavating the land beneath and piling the topsoil up around the perimeter. Straw bales were then stacked in the space created to accommodate the height and shape required for the internal cavity. The next step was to pour mass concrete into the void between the soil banks and the straw. After it had set, the earth was removed, to reveal a single amorphous form resembling an enormous rock. The surrounding soil had transformed the concrete, lending it the texture and color of natural stone. It was then sliced open to reveal the cavity. For the final and perhaps most unorthodox step, a calf named Paulina was housed in The Truffle. Over the course of the following year, Paulina consumed all the straw, allowing the interior to be transformed into a monastic bolthole that combines the spirit of Le Corbusier's Cabanon with the look and feel of a sea cave.

THE RED HOUSE

The art collector owner of this unusual London townhouse in a nineteenth-century conservation area in Chelsea wanted the building itself to be a standalone work of art, as well as a place to display his collection of contemporary works. The brief required a unique design in keeping with the history of the heritage site. Built from concrete clad in a screen of French red limestone, the Red House slots harmoniously in beside its red-brick neighbors, despite its strikingly modern—and deliberately austere—frontage. Windows made from bronze drawn onto timber punctuate the facade, while a red-stone sliding door conceals a garage on the first floor. An entrance court beside the garage leads through to a double-height entrance hall that overlooks a garden filled with lush palm trees, an arresting contrast to the stark exterior that faces the street. Inside, each level of the townhouse has been imbued with a different atmosphere. The ground floor draws on the spatial characteristics of early Modernism, culminating in a glazed dining pavilion set within the garden. Upstairs, a large Italianate room accommodates the owner's art collection, opening onto a balcony overlooking the historic buildings of the surrounding neighborhood. A mezzanine level houses a narrow study, while above, the bedrooms and bathrooms are arranged around a peaceful and densely planted roof terrace.

C4L

The exterior walls of C4L, constructed by pouring concrete into a bamboo framework, set the tone for this three-story Tokyo home. A slender pool borders an artfully lit walkway that leads to the front door; inside, the first-floor living area features walkways carved from natural stone, with areas beneath them covered in rubble. Here, stone and timber combine to celebrate the warmth and artistry of the many handmade elements.

Based in Roppongi, Tokyo, Cubo Design Architect / Hitoshi Saruta wanted to create a restful environment that combined Japanese sensibilities with a diverse mix of influences from other cultures. They drew on traditional ideas around light and shadow to

enhance textural and artisanal details, as well as the concept of *wabi-sabi*, a centuries-old approach that recognizes the beauty of impermanence and imperfection.

More polished spaces can be found on the upper floors, where the palette of wood and stone continues, albeit in more refined forms. The spacious master bedroom and bathroom are a highlight. Here, a low-lying platform bed is screened by delicate braided cords, while the vast en suite features a sunken stone bath. On the top floor, a kitchen and dining area flows out to a south-facing terrace that serves as a tranquil outdoor living space.

HOUSE B

Situated next to a tree-lined pond, in a former castle garden in the suburbs of Antwerp, this austere Belgian home has been designed to find harmony with nature. The exterior of House B is clad in slabs of *muschelkalk*, a type of limestone with a brownish-gray hue, which DDM Architectuur selected for its propensity to weather beautifully over time. They wanted a material with textural and tonal variations that would adapt to the changing light and to the seasonal colors of the surrounding foliage. The polished *muschelkalk* panels are arranged in three different sizes in a directionless Roman pattern so that the roof surfaces and facades merge into one another. Beneath them,

generous windows form the walls to much of the interior, offering wraparound views of water and woodland. The meandering floor plan capitalizes on these views, while allowing natural light to permeate the spaces throughout the day. On the ground floor is an open-plan kitchen and living area, as well as a wellness space comprising a swimming pool and sauna. Bedrooms and a double-height music room are also on this level, while the second floor boasts a library, and a master bedroom that looks out to the treetops. Outside, rough stone slabs form a succession of stepping stones and terraces that provide a visual link between the angular forms of the building and its bucolic setting.

XEROLITHI

Dwarfed by an impressive rock formation that dominates a steep incline scattered with thorn bushes, this inconspicuous Greek home, which winds across a hillside on the island of Serifos, takes its cues from ancient dry stone walls. Sinas Architects conceived the design for Xerolithi to help camouflage it within the island environment, where these walls — known locally as *louria* or *xerolithies* — create terraced strips of farmland that cut across the sloping terrain. When they embarked on this project, the Athens-based practice looked to alternative forms of archetypal Cycladic architecture for ideas that would allow the house to blend seamlessly with its surroundings. The traditional dry stone wall became a starting point, leading to

a concept with facades formed by *xerolithies* that rise and fall in a semi-parallel fashion. Long and slender, the ribbon-like structure is topped with a dirt roof complete with native planting, to better conceal the house within the stepped terraces. Most of the construction material was excavated from the site, supplemented by stone quarried on the nearby island of Paros. The timber pergola, used both inside and out, is another vernacular element referenced by Sinas Architects. These bamboo-topped structures cover the ceilings of the serene, white-walled rooms, and bridge the void between the main home and the separate guesthouse, maintaining the unbroken, flow that allows this home to weave so sinuously across the landscape.

THE LAYER

Designed for an elderly couple returning home after many years abroad, this South Korean house has been conceived as a series of horizontal layers. Seoul-based practice OBBA wanted the residence to be a welcoming, practical, and comfortable second home making the most of its idyllic plot, located at the foot of Mount Toema, one hour northwest of Seoul, overlooking a vast reservoir.

Five walls built from angular blocks of stone delineate the layout of the single-story building, which contains no stairs. The walls cut through the house, carving up the floor plan into different sections for sleeping, relaxing, cooking, and dining. Each area is defined by different dimensions, materials, and textures, according to its purpose, with parts of the interior featuring the same rough-hewn stone used for the facade.

The visual effect of the layered concept is particularly effective when experienced from the long, wide corridor that runs through the center of the house, separating mixed-use zones within each open-plan section, and designed to enhance the couple's enjoyment of the house as they pass through its various spaces. One side of the home opens up to pocket gardens sheltered by the protruding walls; the other embraces views toward the mountains and reservoir: an ever-present reminder of the peace and remoteness that drew the owners to the location.

CASA PIEDRA

Set on a peninsular on the south side of Acapulco Bay, this clifftop home perches high above the ocean on an ancient granite outcrop. Two gargantuan boulders are central to the design of the house, which protrudes from the rocky terrain and achieves harmony with the natural environment, despite its clean lines and sharp edges. Mexican studio Taller Gabriela Carrillo faced multiple challenges building on this site, foremost to preserve the spirit that defines the landscape. The simple grid-like structure is made solely from colored concrete—a mix of local sand and cement—that emulates the warm tones of the granite boulders. Its design accommodates the contours of the hillside, and comprises a series of spaces that open up to the outdoors, with only a few areas fully enclosed. From outside, the four-story house has no clearly defined front or back, and the natural surroundings are given equal importance. The confident simplicity of the scheme feeds into the goal of keeping architectural intervention to a minimum, allowing views of the pool, sea, and jungle to shape the spaces within. Bedrooms and living areas are located above or around the large infinity pool; here, terraces have been strategically positioned across the expansive plot to maximize views and create a dialogue with the enveloping natural world.

BRIONE HOUSE

Located above the city of Locarno, on the shores of Lake Maggiore, this restrained Swiss home is a purposefully discreet response to the crowded hillside on which it sits. Local practice Wespi de Meuron Romeo Architects conceived the home as two simple granite cubes emerging from the hill and opening up to views of the mountains and lake.

The aim was to create a house in keeping with the landscape, rather than to associate it with the nearby residential buildings; a structure more akin to a rugged drystone wall than any conventional representation of a home. Local granite was sourced for its construction, some reclaimed from derelict houses in the area, while flagstones salvaged from a former church were used for the floors.

Two large openings, each screened by a gridded wooden gate, break up the facades of the stacked volumes. On the lower level, a parking garage with a dramatic sloping wall provides access to the two-story house that sits above it, where a pool embedded in the lower volume stretches out to meet the horizon. Inside, the design reflects the simplicity of the exterior, allowing the scenery and stone construction to remain front and center. Cleverly positioned courtyards draw light into the house, without compromising the air of seclusion that defines this quietly luxurious hideaway.

ROGAČ HOUSE

This four-story home on the Croatian island of Vis in the Adriatic Sea rises up from a steep slope above the harbor like a fortress. Designed by Split-based Studio Archaos, Rogač House is built from coarsely chiseled local stone and takes inspiration from an ancient tower in the town below. The choice of stone is a reference to the island's historic building traditions, and finds an easy synergy with the contemporary honed concrete that is used for the terraces, balconies, entrance bridge, and roof. A thoughtful arrangement of windows, both large and small, punctures the exterior on three sides, affording different vistas of sea, sky, and the ancient carob trees that lend the house its name, without compromising privacy. The rear of the villa, which flanks the steep hillside, is almost completely devoid of openings; here, a concrete bridge provides access by car and on foot, its elevation dictated by the incline of the slope, as well as local building regulations. A master bedroom and bathroom occupy the top floor of the house, leading out onto a roof terrace that capitalizes on views over the bay. Two additional bedrooms are located on the floor below, while an open-plan kitchen, living, and dining space can be found beneath. The ground level is dedicated to wine storage, as well as an outdoor kitchen overlooking the swimming pool, which is shaded by the terrace above.

SUN VALLEY HOUSE

Blending seamlessly with the muted shades of its spectacular backdrop, this mountain home retreat in the northwestern state of Idaho immerses its owners in nature throughout the changing seasons. Situated at the base of Ruud Mountain in Sun Valley, the house consists of two wings constructed from local small-rubble granite and zinc that appear to slide together and pull apart. The volumes slope away from one another creating a profile that traces the outline of the distant peaks, and a sense of unity between house and landscape.

Every room has been positioned to frame a different view, taking in the changing colors of the awe-inspiring scenery, which is blanketed by snow in winter, when the area transforms into a popular skiing destination. The interior feels perfectly in keeping with a mountain bolthole: exposed wooden ceiling beams, solid-wood floors, and enormous hearths built from the same small-rubble granite as the exterior. The two wings separate the private and communal areas, while guest accommodation is located below, set into the mountainside. Outside, a partially covered north-facing terrace offers a quiet spot to relax by the outdoor fireplace. From here, stairs lead up to a hidden roof terrace with panoramic views, where the owners can sleep beneath the stars in summer.

CM HOUSE

Local studio Además Arquitectura faced constraints on both shape and materials, including a stipulation for a pitched roof, when designing this family home located within a golf and country club on the outskirts of Buenos Aires. In response to the limitations, the architects explored the archetypal shape of a house, developing a concept with two separate volumes, each with a hip-roofed design. Entirely clad in pale and textural travertine, the walls and roofs appear as a single element, offering a contemporary twist on a familiar form. The larger of the volumes—containing the bedrooms, a gym, and a poolside living space—is laid out across two floors, the upper level of which cantilevers over a glazed facade that leads out to the garden. The second volume—a separate single-story building—reinterprets the *quincho*, a traditional domestic and social space where the family gathers to cook on a charcoal grill, normally detached from the main house. A fresh take on a traditional concept, the studio felt that fragmenting the different interior spaces would increase the connection between the indoor and outdoor areas, allowing the owners to make the most of the verdant surroundings.

REDHILL BARN

This once-dilapidated nineteenth-century threshing barn and cowshed occupies an isolated corner of farmland in Devon in the southwest of England. London architectural practice TYPE were tasked with transforming the impressive agricultural relic into a sustainable home, to serve as the hub of a new 25-acre (10.1-hectare) ecological smallholding. Intent on preserving the original walls of the ramshackle barn, the studio designed and retrofitted a home within the existing shell, retaining the character of the architecture and weathered stone construction. Doors and windows were fitted into the existing openings in the thick walls, set back to bring maximum light to the interior. A simple hipped roof made from milled aluminum sheeting was chosen to mimic the original roof form, its corrugated profile and gutterless design a reference to utilitarian agricultural architecture. Inside, the original stone columns support a new timber floor, and the visible roof structure makes full use of the height of the space. Conceived as a series of floating boxes spread across two levels, TYPE aimed to create livable, intimate spaces without detracting from the structure and scale that had previously defined the interior of the barn. Upstairs, an open-plan space is dedicated to living and working; on the first floor, two bedrooms and the kitchen take advantage of the many arched doors—originally intended for cattle—that connect the home with the countryside that surrounds it.

STONE COURT VILLA

Set in a sprawling, 10-acre (4-hectare) stretch of the Sonoran Desert in Paradise Valley, this four-bedroom Arizona home is comprised of limestone volumes arranged around a series of courtyards, blurring the boundaries between outside and in. Conceived by Los Angeles-based practice MASASTUDIO, it is constructed from Veracruz Mexican saw-cut limestone bricks that complement the bleached hues of the arid terrain. The pale limestone walls are laid out in a repetitive yet complex manner, achieving a reassuring uniformity and referencing the profiles of the distant mountain peaks that dwarf the low-lying villa. At certain points, the walls have been extended to create enclosed terraces, some of which are shaded by canopies of delicate fabric. The exterior and interior spaces are organized around a dominant central courtyard, while a large swimming pool separates the master bedroom from the guest accommodation. Inspiration for the stacked-stone construction came from an eclectic combination of sources, including a Japanese bamboo chopping board and the grid-like work of American Abstract Expressionist painter Agnes Martin. The design is enhanced by the subtle tactility of the sawn stone, which changes in tone and texture as the desert light changes throughout the day. Some of the walls include perforated sections that filter the sun and create delicate shadows inside and out.

CASA TAPIHUE

Surrounded by vines in the valley of Tapihue, in Casablanca, this sprawling stone home in Chile's wine-growing region is the work of Santiago-based practice Matías Zegers Arquitectos. Designed in collaboration with Chilean architect Catalina Pacheco, the concept of this vineyard home comprises four volumes built from white stone arranged around a central courtyard. Intended to shelter the inhabitants from the area's strong winds, the scheme invites them to enjoy the landscape stretching out in all directions. The house sits on a concrete plinth approximately 3 ft (0.9 m) above ground level, to afford a better view across the vineyards. Despite its enclosed formation, large windows ensure that sight lines flow from the courtyard through the house and out to the valley beyond. A large library dominates one side of the home, with open wooden shelving allowing unbroken views through the space, which contains the main living and dining areas. Natural materials feature throughout, complementing the interior stone walls that slice through the house, a fluid extension of the external structure of the building. Timber ceilings add warmth, while smooth concrete floors and walls contrast with the pale and tactile masonry that serves as a rustic counterpoint to the streamlined, fuss-free furniture and joinery.

CRUACHAN BEAG

Set on a spectacular promontory on the Isle of Eriskay in Scotland, this two-roomed bothy has evolved from the ruins of an old stone structure that stood on the site. Once a home, and later perhaps a dairy shed, the building had undergone numerous adaptations before being left to the mercy of the elements on the rocky outcrop. When Glasgow-based practice BARD set about transforming it into a livable island bolthole, their aim was to retain the familiar essence of the many enigmatic small stone buildings scattered across rural Scotland.

The project is simple in concept and construction, with a timber frame inserted within the original walls, which were built from Lewisian gneiss rock. Compact and considered, the interior comprises a modest kitchen, a wall bed that can be stowed away during the day, and a shower room with a floor-to-ceiling window slotted into an existing opening in the stonework.

The main living space is vaulted, and punctured with large windows to leverage the majesty of a view that takes in the sea, sky, and rugged coastline. To let the morning light in to the bothy, east-facing roof lights have been installed in the new roof, which is clad in Ballachulish slates salvaged from another of the studio's Hebridean projects. Cruachan Beag is a masterclass in sensitive restoration that pays respect to the past as well as the landscape.

INDEX

Phaidon Press Limited
2 Cooperage Yard
London E15 2QR

Phaidon Press Inc.
111 Broadway
New York, NY 10006

phaidon.com

First published 2024
© 2024 Phaidon Press Limited

ISBN 978 1 83866 904 1

A CIP catalogue record for this book is available
from the British Library and the Library of Congress.

Commissioning Editor: Emilia Terragni
Project Editor: Rosie Pickles
Text: Tessa Pearson
Production Controller: Lily Rodgers
Design: Studio Chehade

Printed in China

Picture credits

Architettura Urbana: 44, 47b; Luis Asín: 76, 77, 78, 79; © ARS, NY and DACS, London 2024 / Will Ashley / Shutterstock: 119; Alex Attard: 110, 111, 112, 113; Iwan Baan: 174, 176–177; BARD: 234; Cesar Bejar: 40, 41, 42, 43; Nathanael Bennett: 104, 105, 106–107, 108, 109; Benjamin Benschneider: 137t, 137b, 138, 140; Hélène Binet: 178, 181; Jeremy Bitterman: 214, 215, 216t; Bosnic+Dorotic: 210, 211, 212, 213; Javier Callejas: 54, 55, 56, 57; Juan Sanchez Calventus: 170, 171, 172, 173; Tomeu Canyellas: 124, 125, 126, 127; Paulo Catrica: 94, 95, 96, 97, 98, 99; Daniel Joseph Chenin: 12, 13t; Peter Clarke: 71, 74, 75; Peter Cooke: 179, 180; Johan Dehlin: 66, 67, 68, 69; Dwight Eschliman: 136, 139, 141; Jose Elias / StockPhotosArt – Urban Landscape / Alamy Stock Photo: 50, 51; Joe Fletcher: 216b, 217, 226, 227, 228, 229; Rafael Gamo: 200, 201, 202, 203t, 203b; Rory Gardiner: 222, 223, 224, 225; Amit Geron: 20, 21, 22, 23, 24–25; GHA: 46, 47t; Dan Glasser: 132, 133, 134–135, 166, 167, 168, 169; Piet-Albert Goethals: 36, 37, 38, 39; Joan Guillamat: 58, 59, 60–61; Roland Halbe: 175; Hannes Henz Architekturfotograf: 204, 205, 206, 207, 208, 209; Ben Hosking: 146, 147, 148–149, 150, 151; Ivo Tavares Studio: 142, 143, 144, 145; Alexander James-Aylin: 235, 236, 237; Rick Joy: 216b; Courtesy KKA: 26, 27, 28–29; © Koji Fujii / TOREAL: 182, 183, 184, 185; Yiorgos Kordakis: 190, 191, 192–193, 194, 195; Kyungsub Shin: 196, 197t, 197b, 198, 199t, 199b; © Edmon Leong: 80, 81, 82, 83; Lenzer: 186, 187, 188, 189; Maciej Lulko: 62, 63, 64–65; Giorgio Marafioti: 114, 115, 116, 117; Fernando Marroquin: 128, 129, 130, 131; Stephen Morgan: 13b; James Morris: 162, 163, 164, 165; Cristóbal Palma: 230, 231, 232, 233; Sergio Pirrone: 90, 91, 92–93; Eugeni Pons: 16, 17, 18, 19; Bharath Ramamrutham: 84, 85, 86, 87, 88, 89; Ana Santl: 30, 31, 32, 33, 34, 35; StockPhotosArt / Shutterstock: 52–53; © ARS, NY and DACS, London 2024 / akg-images / VIEW Pictures / Grant Smith: 120; Christopher Sturman: 156, 157, 158–159, 160, 161; Derek Swalwell: 70, 72, 73; TEd'A arquitectes: 100, 101, 102, 103; © ARS, NY and DACS, London 2024 / Frank Tozier / Alamy Stock Photo: 121; © ARS, NY and DACS, London 2024 / Michael Ventura / Alamy Stock Photo: 118; Gonzalo Viramonte: 218, 219, 220, 221; Panagiotis Voumvakis: 154t, 154b, 155; © ARS, NY and DACS, London 2024 / Daniel Wilson / Alamy Stock Photo: 122–123; Stetson Ybarra: 10, 11, 14–15; Yiorgis Yerolymbos: 152, 153; Andrea Zanchi Photography: 45, 48–49.